THE SIEGE OF MONROVIA

- a poem -

Mark Huband

Photographs: Patrick Robert

LIVE CANON

First Published in 2017
By Live Canon Ltd
www.livecanon.com

All rights reserved

© Mark Huband 2017

978-1-909703-15-5 (Hardback)
978-1-909703-16-2 (Paperback)

The right of Mark Huband to be identified as author of this work has been asserted by him in accordance with Section 77 of the Copyright, Design and Patents Act 1988.

All rights reserved. No part of this publication may be reproduced, stored in or introduced into a retrieval system, or transmitted, in any form, or by any means (electronic, mechanical, photocopying, recording or otherwise) without the prior written permission of the publisher. Any person who does any unauthorized act in relation to this publication may be liable to criminal prosecution and civil claims for damages.

A CIP catalogue record for this book is available from the British Library.

This book is sold subject to the condition that it shall not, by way of trade or otherwise, be lent, re-sold, hired out, or otherwise circulated without the publisher's prior consent in any form of binding or cover other than that in which it is published and without a similar condition including this condition being imposed on the subsequent purchaser.

Photographs: Patrick Robert

Edited by Helen Eastman for Live Canon
www.livecanon.co.uk
@livecanon

THE SIEGE OF MONROVIA

Born on the Yorkshire moors, Mark Huband grew up in Harlow, Essex. As a journalist and author he spent twenty-five years travelling the world. Postings as a newspaper correspondent in Abidjan and Nairobi took him to most countries of sub-Saharan Africa as they emerged from the Cold War. Initially for the *Financial Times* and then as Africa correspondent for the *Guardian* and the *Observer*, he covered the civil war in Liberia, the famine in Somalia, genocide in Rwanda and Burundi, and the conflicts in Angola and Sudan. Moving to Morocco, his focus was the emergence of political Islam across North Africa and the Middle East. Rebasing to Cairo as regional correspondent for the *Financial Times*, he became immersed in the turmoil stretching from Afghanistan to Algeria. Moving to London, in the wake of the 11 September 2001 terrorist attacks he was appointed to oversee the *FT*'s coverage of Al-Qaida – a role which took him from the slums of Manila to the prison at Guantanamo Bay.

The author of eight books on Africa, the Middle East and global affairs, his debut collection of poetry, American Road, was published by Live Canon in 2014, and has been followed by publication in several anthologies and a pamphlet, Skinny White Kids (2017).

www.markhuband.com

Introduction

In 1989 a young foreign correspondent, looking to make a name for himself, set off for a new life in West Africa. Writing initially for the *Financial Times* and subsequently for *The Guardian*, Mark Huband travelled far and wide, from the tumult of Mobutu's Zaïre to the Saharan homeland of the Touaregs, telling the stories of West Africa during that tumultuous time as the Cold War came to an end.

When a small group of Libyan-trained fighters crossed the border into Liberia on Christmas Eve 1989, the series of wars which followed tore Liberia to pieces. Ostensibly launched to bring an end to the ten-year dictatorship of Liberia's President Samuel Doe, the ensuing decade of bloodshed left the country brutalised, its people traumatised, and its economy ruined.

Rebel factions formed around Charles Taylor, a renegade government minister, and Prince Johnson, a former government soldier who broke away from Taylor's National Patriotic Front of Liberia. Characterised by the use of child soldiers, rape, drug-fuelled violence, and tribal slaughter, the Liberian civil war rapidly lost its purpose of liberating Liberians from dictatorship.

Mark Huband was the first journalist to reach behind rebel lines, and reported on the war from all sides. Most journalists left when Monrovia, Liberia's capital city, was besieged by both rebel factions in the summer of 1990. Mark remained for the three months that the city was under attack, and his award-winning journalism provided a unique account of the conflict and its atrocities.

But it is only now, almost thirty years later, that Mark has been able to write his own personal account of that time he spent among the rebels, killers, victims and warlords. He has found a way to do this in poetry, the terza rima form of the narrative poem *The Siege of Monrovia* allowing the verse to speak the unspeakable and describe the indescribable, in a work which bears witness to a time of chaos and bloodshed, but which also has space for light and humanity.

The powerful photos which illustrate the text are the work of Patrick Robert, with whom Mark often travelled, and who has fearlessly photographed numerous conflicts in the course of an exceptional career. Explore more of his work at http://www.patrick-robert.com/.

Dr Helen Eastman (Editor)

For Tom Hammick

THE SIEGE OF MONROVIA

Prologue

Summer. 1990. Early in June
the war had reached the city's suburbs.
Yards chained. Gates slammed. It will be over soon.

Fear is a suitcase splayed at the kerb
of a rain-sheen road. Telegraph poles bow
low, wires ripped, lines down. Voices once heard

soft-whisper last words. A road's gentle brow
echoes of a place, now a gaping mouth,
which hums the sun-moon tune bare feet follow

as bait. Once, the beach paths which wound down south
were soft as the shadows of breeze-blown fronds.
Nobody goes there now, a rumoured truth

telling murmured tales of how beyond
the beach-huts dogs now gnaw the flesh from bones.

*

Rocking in the strobe of a churning storm
which prowls the forest edge and mangrove shore,
a plane skims the day's growling sky. Rain, warm,

claws the runway. Scarred men wait for war
to come, passports thumbed, lip-mouthed words snarl numb,
the question: 'What is your mission here?'

And there is no answer. 'Why have you come
to watch us die? What do you want of us,
now all we thought we had has finally gone?'

Ghosts of men. Silver-badged, gold braid, holsters
at the hip, old NYPD dreaming
fantastic tales of shared histories.

The saviour's orphaned step-child is screaming:
'Save us'. But the saviour is not listening.

And in the hollow of a nightmare swept
on dawn's cool cusp, shapes loom at windows,
drawn by an imagined hand which once crept

ragged through savage darkness. Mosquitoes
suck night's salt skin. And in the light of dawn
this storyteller saw his past now close

with the sunrise, his past a place to mourn,
a past which would not wake again – till now,
when out of death he would see life still-born

on this land, as he tried to tell of how
by chance he came upon a war. No past
to look upon, he became somehow

the aimless chronicler, at times outcast,
on the loneliest voyage tied to a mast.

Earth twists in shard streams where the dust-light falls,
the voice of footsteps the waking of day
like no other day, beyond the walls

which bound the storyteller where he lay.
Strange witness. But he's another story,
all silence, as he woke and made his way

into the light of morning. His story
lay in the silence of the tale which tells
of how he once was warned: do not weary

readers with old tales. So a silence falls,
and those who may once have listened are gone,
far from where day now warms the shanty walls

deep in a forest where a pigeon's song
is of a garden where his dreams belong.

*

Fire bit deep as the men raged their oaths
of blood and death by the roadside. Strangers
and countrymen hacked stumps of men, clothed

by token charms to repel ghost dangers
conjured from the spellbound myths of folklore
passed on milk-tongued laughter sour as juice.

Their sounds became the melody of war.
Brick charred to cinder, iron, rust, warm rain
a soft power in a land without lore,

without love, without words. The rain again,
knotting mist drapes with earth's mortal moment.
Some order yelled, shots uttered in vain

among the trees, where good spirits lament:
'The Country Devil might never repent'.

Rumour had it that the Devil was killed,
knifed by a boy somewhere near Saklepié.
True or not, the story spread far afield

by whisper in the humming drumming day,
on breath stale as if time had breathed the
lingering stench of chaos, all the way

along the coastline to Monrovia.
The Devil was dead, a boy in his place
a savage in the guise of believer,

playing chief and sage, a mask for a face,
his junkie-fire courage burning rage.
See, the eyes which no longer leave their trace

on the boy without memory or age,
a wordless child outcast on a stage.

First Part: Strangers

The calm-eyed, sad *New York Times* reporter
offers a ride from Spriggs Payne airfield –
from the stained-wood desk rubber-stamp clamour

of the smeared hallway where men could wield
power's final strokes. This time the last time,
or perhaps one last deal might be sealed

before the last dollar clenches the last palm
and then one morning the last flight is flown.
Outside, flags limp in the rain, morning warm

like any other day, the salt-sea blown
across what once were streets now turned to beats
of tip-toe feet creeping past the sweat-stone

eyes of checkpoint guards. All along the street
eyes spy the bodies to trick or to treat.

The *Times* man is gone, beyond the scarred gate
of a villa by the beach, shoulders hunched
beneath a sports holdall which bears the weight

of his assignment. On the breeze the stench
of rotting rolls with the waves. Like the sea,
a glimpse of the sea, watching rollers wrench

the shoreline from its roots, as in the lee
the breeze spits salt in the eyes of a bitch
which drags her blind pups, and his own story

turns and turns, twisting broke upon waves which
now growl beneath his storyteller's breath.
The light is shapes now, and the air is rich

with stale fires and hunger's scent, with
past's torn page and the hollow toll of faith.

*

The car echoes the tunnel of the road.
City of ditches, rust shacks, cleaved signboards,
wastelands to cross, seeping walls, a truck's load

scattered in the gutter of checkpoint words
spun false as power: 'Halt. Halt I say. Halt.
What you got for me?' as fists clench triggers,

punching gun metal, the click of a bolt,
that rot-stench again, from beyond a wall,
as rage eyes feed on the wounds of the cult:

'Declare yourself white man.' Then play the role,
speak of nowhere, give no sign, no loose word
to wrench the spine. Neither swagger nor stroll.

Invisible now. Hear what can be heard,
after the silence has drained the last word

called along streets which meet at the crossroads.
The taxis are deep yellow. Food for sale
at street stalls, and a carter now unloads

a fridge, a cooker, leaves of purple kale.
Like signs of life. Perhaps celebrating
all that once was, all gone upon the gale

now twisting southward, creeping stealth, writhing
in shapeless consciousness, now a spirit
women hear, children sing, which men now cling

to as they step beyond the sunlight
into nightmare myth. A policeman blows
a whistle to halt the traffic, his white

gloves starch crisp, as the storyteller goes
on his way to a place where noon-light glows

on a body drowsing in the half-light
of a curtained room in a duplex block.
She stirs, sheets tangling skin, warm breath so slight

upon the pillow. The tick of a clock
and breath rising falling, are time's soft beat,
the ocean's rush now froth among the rocks

which rip the tide outside beyond the street.
Breath rising falling, she carries the weight
of their child, there, where rock and water meet.

'It cannot be, can never be our fate,'
he tells himself, but then tells her only:
'You must leave this place before it's too late,'

and sees his story as it might have been
and leaves alone what he might once have seen

on the street, where a voice calls: 'Where yer been?
Watch yer step. Better take care. Everyone
knows about you in the forest, that train

the rebels hit. Say, d'ja bring whiskey, man?
A hundred bucks a bottle here. Shit.
What a shithole this place is. Ain't no-one

gonna tell me different.' And a gunshot
cracks the soft warm air. A generator
belches smoke. A girl screams. A bullet hits

the Stars and Stripes at a balcony door
and waves slap the beach. 'Got a fresh body
down on the sand. White man. Ain't like before.

They got a white man,' and the white foam's rush
turns and turns fat bleached limbs and fresh cut flesh

dragging the sands near the Ambassador
Pizzeria the owner plans to close
because the city has changed, changing for

the worse, 'Not like it used to be. Who knows
if they'll sort it out. I'm not waiting here
to see. That body, they took all his clothes.

Go see. Looks white. Now we're all in fear.
Before, they left us alone. But it's white,
that body. They never did that before.

Kept us out of it.' And as raw sun bites
with midday light, the diners wipe their lips,
settle bills, amble curious in spite

of themselves. Just looking, as salt-sea slips
in, slips out. Where a head turned, darkness gapes

deep in the hollow salt-sea emptiness
no face had ever seen before that time,
like the early days, before timelessness

traced the city by rain by sun's noon-time
till there was no time, and Peabody told
the driver: 'A little more. It's no crime.

A last chance to see my home.' Rain whips cold
as Peabody – sage and pressman – drives us out
into the eastern suburbs, past the old

homes of the freed slave settlers, to Duport
Road. 'My home,' Peabody says, where a park
between villas is seed-grass now. A cat

prowls tall blades, tip-toeing skulls, eyes dark
as the black-rain road which nobody walks,

and we drive again, and see no movement but
our own, no stir of life, there where rain falls
and the sun has no world to warm, just light

which glares, greasing its sheen upon green walls
guarding a garden's ghastly emptiness.
There was ritual then. But then it passes

into a stolen second's wilderness
moment. All is gone. All is horizon.
All is bone. Hunger raw as the dreamless

hour, when she left by the last flight, on
the last plane to crawl into the thunder.

She left me there, two stories now undone
as tales of paths once crossed, left to wonder
what we might have been to one another.

Second Part: Papa

So quiet, the afternoon street. Which day
might this be? I have been walking these streets
for so many days now, they drift away

on the rotting trash tip which oozes sweet
sunlit dappled shade up the dead-end lane
beside my duplex block, where troops now meet

and talk and stride and muster and explain
nothing but fear as they disappear
inside a house, and then emerge again

and sit a man between them in their car.
And then drive. And I watch the man turning
his head from side to side. And see neither

soldier speak, not turning nor speaking.
On the way to kill. That's where they take him,

from the house on the lane I step inside.
Step inside. And there are his children,
sat in a row on wooden chairs beside

a shelf of photos, their faces wracked,
hands crossed neat on prim-pressed school uniforms,
young faces screaming, bare legs kicking,

the skin of slapped faces now bruised by hands
helpless to console, helpless to embrace.
'Papa. Papa. Papa. Papa.' The screams

are that room forever, terror that face
turning from side to side. All is terror
now, off the afternoon street, in a place

the world had barely known much of, before
it tore off its clothes and went off to war.

*

So quiet, the afternoon street seeping
now to evening. But there is no night, nor
dawn, no place nor past nor warm eye casting

expectation on next day's blood-cold light
that cuts the walls of painted nowhere rooms.
To hide. To run. To fly upon the light –

the choice mine. Life – ash, brushed by muscled brooms
as dust among the corner interludes
of lives on hold. Children scream in dark rooms

and Papa's tangled writhing solitude
laps rippled darkness on the mangrove swamp
edging the sullen Mesurado's tide,

swelling rumours that in the Barclay Camp
the dead are trophies beneath the salt sand

dragged on the early evening by a breeze
which twists the crests of Atlantic rollers,
which twists the palms wrenched from languorous ease

and the silence of the fun-fair laughter,
of child's play among the Sunday dunes
now fresh-dug. Fallen fronds crack where softer

sand lies as dust among parched wind-wept bones,
dog-ripped dry, ant-picked clean. The salt carves jaws
silent as fun-fair laughter, soft as stone

hauled on currents the spit-sea's lash now claws
beside the Barclay Camp, as a shot cuts
the fun-fair swings, boots run and a voice roars:

'What you see?' and the air is filled with shots,
and I run on salt breath among rust huts.

*

But I cannot cry, nor know the fear
I must feel. I am no more than rain.
I am no more than the storyteller

forgotten by the story told in vain
by strangers, whose brief moments were their own
until they were the folklore they became,

until they were the stories none had known,
till I passed by and came across the dead
and saw the place where I might die alone,

in the drowned-sound ditch-hut rust-rattling
of writhing storms. Perhaps this is the place
I came to die and then be born again

as some other. I am gone without trace
upon soft light towards days-end's embrace

in the distant moan of crawling thunder
which groans the agony of wrenched red earth,
then roars the voice of the drowned land's trauma.

Then it passes, sloping with rain-tin breath,
north into the forest. But with the sun
there is no next moment, no word to soothe

the Carey Street gang outside *El Meson*,
some-time soldiers barring the speakeasy
door with eyes of ice and clattering guns

slung over skinny shoulders. 'An' for me?'
a sergeant rasps, a threat, a plea. 'ID –
where your ID?' I shove past, will not see

the eye that catches mine, won't pay a fee
to close the door on what lurks behind me.

Spirits glow glass behind the bar, sweet scents
rich, wet on the lip-beat breathing mumbled
talk of war which creeps across a distance

some say may be no more than a fumbled
clock's last chime away, no more than the next
storm's raging hour before it stumbles

against the street door, the cool inside flexed
in shadow by the stares of cold dark eyes
beneath a helmet's brim. Soldiers stare, fixed

on spying an enemy in the glow
of the bar-room light, the *New York Times* man
catching their eye, his black skin all they know
as proof 'he on rebel side, and now go
to the Barclay Camp, we carry you so

let's go now. We carry you.' So they try
to take him to the street outside, away
from the rum-sweet murmur and drunken sighs

of white men with nowhere to run, who stay
to watch the war from balconies above
the wet streets where to walk is to fall prey

to savage fear. A diplomat arrives,
combed and trim among the growl of armed men
at the bar, and pressed shirt neat has the *Times*

man follow him to his car and unharmed
to a plane to far away from here.
And the chatter resumes and nerves are calmed

and stone-faced the waiter now glides over,
boasts: 'Our lobster's the best in Monrovia.'

And so we eat. Slug ice-cold beer. Fumble
with the cruet set. Rearrange paper
napkins, knives, forks, as the waiter mumbles

the dessert list. 'Will it be your desire
to take coffee?' We nod and then chuckle
and embarrassed he straightens his bow-tie,

edges stiff-backed to the kitchen, cracked skull
skin choked by the grip of his frayed collar.
'Bring us more beer,' the *Reuters* man calls

after him. He nods. 'Ice-cold, you hear?'
'Ice-cold beer, and this lobster's quite good,'
the *Associated Press* reporter

ponders, smirking over his plate of food,
glancing to where the ice-cold waiter stood

in the shadow of the soldiers' gaze. And
it's cool in there, and maybe safe inside.
We could stay in there, hide away for days

and nights upstairs above the street outside,
where the balcony girls laugh pidgin calls
as we leave the waiter sweating blood-eyed.

'What d'ja do here?' The balcony girls
shout back: 'We make love'. And they laugh and laugh
and the soldiers grin and the street echoes

for a lost moment, and the street is safe
like the bar beyond the door. Then the street
is empty as the rain on every breath,

as clammy as the fear-sweat, now sweet
as laughter drowning in the rain's blind beat

upon the door night has closed behind me.
Descend the concrete steps into sunlight.
Pace slow. Pace fast. What might this next day be

dreaming it will be? Blue sky near-white,
caught in a glance, creeps the oil-black street.
Step onto the dark street, sun without light

now casting all into timeless silence
but for the wanderer's hungry breath I draw
on the corner of UN Drive, where once

a man sold beer and gold tequila
and ham and pasta – everything for cash:
'No credit these days' – and Coca-Cola:

'Gimme a soda'. Now his shop is trashed,
the street dead rooms where time's bones rot a gashed

leg melting to the trash on which it died,
twisted down an alley, maybe hidden,
maybe running on hungry breath inside

a home just out of reach. A sudden
rattle, fingers running over a blind,
a snare drum struck, the sound of wooden

shoes upon a stair. Bats scream the anthem
of those times, soaring ragged in a swarm,
alone free to cruise the skies. A rhythm

mumbles from behind a curtain, a warm
voice sings loud into the desolation,
the player risking all without a qualm

as I pass and wonder who sang that song,
learning only after that time had gone,

humming paced alley paths between high walls,
a hidden way to the Ducor Hotel,
through a gate beneath the Masons' temple

rising like Rome on Quirinale Hill,
marble ripped, columns torn, a fantasy
the lone dictator has tried so hard to kill,

its skeleton dome now ribs, a rusty
hollow against the drifting peaks of clouds.
Trees sway the sweep of the hotel driveway

where kings and presidents once waved to crowds.
Now, carcass cars clutter the lot, waiting
for owners long-fled, cars beneath dust shrouds

safe at the hotel, its five-star rating
a boast, a hope that this war is fleeting.

Frogs lurch the gutter-tiled swimming pool,
trash clogging drains where the elite once swam
through the days of another time, ice cool

under parasol shade. Mosquitoes swarm.
The poolside bar is firewood. Beyond
the terrace with the ocean view, smoke worms

into the sky over Bushrod Island.
The view is different now, as Monrovia
slips into the grip of a strangler's hand

and a truck rips every screaming gear
as it flees across the People's Bridge,
crammed with fury, men in terror, hunger-

ravaged, their thirst slaked only by revenge
as fires drag the city to its end,

belched smoke engulfing Cross Street, lights flashing
as a fire truck swerves around the checkpoints,
the men inside calm, eager, responding

to a 9.1.1. just like normal times.
Just a fire. 'No Doe, no Liberia,'
soldiers strutting among the flames they stoke:

'No Doe, no Liberia,' and rounds blaze
the street and flame-eyes rage, and the fire truck
empties of cool rushing water as flames

dance flamenco and the street way beyond
is a molten tail snaking breath, and
the palm street behind once soothed by fronds

is another country in rebel hands,
as the city splits into foreign lands.

Third Part: Thieves

Now may be time to breathe again, along
the tin-can frontier which no one walks
but me. I wonder if this story's one

I'll tell some day, when the city that wakes
now in silence can speak of what it saw
walking the blood-dry streets, as sunlight breaks

night's silent terror into fury's war.
Will all I say be that 'once I was there,
and saw what men can do?' And do I dare

to breathe the death-scent air and still to stare
into the lives of others? I breathe death,
and drift among the ghosts on this street, where

the liberators lounge on striped deck-chairs
and order me over to see what's theirs.

The street is a seeping mouth, the road an eye,
the July day a drum, the light water.
I am moving. I cast a glance, and lie

upon the motion of voices' laughter
spewed from hollow grated deep cackled throats,
guttered as the dank shanks of dogs after

rain. Flash blood eyes catch the pure cloud which floats
alone now free of fear, blood-stone eyes
sunk so deep, away among the remote

swathe swamp which drowned dreams and conjured as lies,
the promise. That promise now rotted teeth
jagged as the grin of spit and smiles

breaking upon ageless skin cracked beneath
the maquillage these gunmen's nightmares weave

into their haunted tales. Never told.
The tale that I too may never tell
was across the street, beneath a crippled

colonnade. I am empty as a shell
of life, in the scarred fisted palm bone grip
of the executioners. Their stares fall

on the stranger whose timeless days now slip
nameless as the emptiness, filling days
with blood-eye rage and the horizon's ripped

seasons, torn shred hours, broken pathways
leading from past to future, as I step
into the shadow of the colonnade

where their prisoners crouch where they have crept
beneath the carcass of a rust-car wreck.

'Thief. Thief. All thieves. All thieves. See what they stole,'
says a chapped-lip mouth, a young face of sweat
speaking of justice. 'Come. See. These men stole

from the people. Come see,' opening with pride
the boot of the rust-wreck car, its remains
the hollow of the journeys it once made.

'See. Look what they took.' Inside, plastic crates
of beer, pink champagne, tinned meat, rusting
cans of haricot vert. A mother waits

to feed a family and a gunman struts
as the law of the land. Eyes turn red rage
on the pleading thieves lying at my feet.

'And now we kill them,' and they set the stage.
'And now we kill them,' and the thieves are caged,

scuttling like crabs beneath the carcass
of the car. What I saw could never be.
Fingers raked a tiled floor, bone and claws

scratching last moments wrung from the day we
now carved from emptiness. I am empty
of words. I am empty of earth. Now I

stand, a vulture around the cowering prey,
my life all there, savage and dumb as stone.
I hear the thieves beneath the car. They cry

and beg, the voices of two men alone
amid the wreckage of the turning world
crawling fast towards their execution.

'And now we kill them,' so the chant is heard.
'And now we kill them,' and the thieves lie curled

beneath the rust upon the oil patch stains,
and plead in holy voices for mercy
as a Kalashnikov shot cracks a pane

of the crippled car and the thieves now cry
as they creep out from the solace shadows
to beg surrender, to conjure mercy

from the raging growl of the fury's flow
which drowns in thunder wild eyes and tongues.
Men. Machines. At my feet. In time as slow

as the fall of leaves. Machines puncture lungs
torn beneath a pink tee-shirt. A leg curls
beneath another. A final breath clings

claw hands, as the executioner flings
ghost words into the dead men's lonely worlds.

The dead lie at my feet. The dead. The dead.
Strangers lie at my feet. Two twisted men.
They died for me. They died for me. I said

nothing to save them from what might happen.
The performance was all for me, the play
a plot of tricks and moves, then a sudden

fury as cruel as the Judgement Day,
when all that might have been is lost, on dust
winding my knotted veins. 'Come. Eat,' they say,

the killers, now slumped on their chairs. 'Man must
eat. Come. Share our rice,' and I smell the twist
of steam from a canteen pan cracked with rust

among the debris of the midday mist,
where fallen blood dries on a dead man's fist.

Crab-hide fingers scoop warm rice from a bowl.
I see them, only now, boys, men. I gaze
in summer light and the darkest shadow

and hope the face they see on me, hope my eyes
do not betray nor my strange words give voice
to the one dying behind my glass haze.

Once upon a time there was no raw choice
between blood and rice. Once upon a time.
Once there was a boy whose words were the noise

of others. So he went away to find
the words he might one day call his own, and
woke into the noise he himself had cried

before his journey brought him to this land,
where now the dregs of rice smear claw hands

which cling the gun metal. This is my home.
Now I am the war. Now, this is my war.
I am the killer with eyes of wet stone,

my life now measured by each breath I draw
on the last moments of the last dry day
I scrape from the street, where I am the law

wrenched from all that was once the memory
I have forgotten I fled to escape.
I am what these men make of the stare I

fix on the shadow where the dead men crept.
I am the dead soul, no story to tell,
no friend in the world, the secret I kept

of a destiny's hand which lied so well,
among dreams now rotting where dead men swell

in the shadow I cast. I am shadow,
a shape catching a sun which caught a face
beside a wall on a street. An unknown,

a figure with no name to call, no trace
of past to frame in words. This is no place.
This is the emptiness, a hollow space

carved from a wasteland. Now, my blood is ice.
I wonder what they see behind my eyes.
I watch their grins, their laughter, hear their cries

of 'halt. You there. Halt and be recognised,'
yelled at the sag taut skin and blood-shot glance
of a man pushing knifed limbs which drape gashed

from a wheelbarrow, its squeak a trance
of rust rhythm on a glitter of glass.

Bone hands loose their grip and the barrow halts.
'This man. Government. He killer. Killer,'
the gunmen yell from their deck-chairs – one shouts:

'Killer. This man. This man,' and his trigger
finger taps at the metal, as he points
at the bleeding man splayed in the barrow,

neither living nor dead. Through a blood squint
of haunted eyes, this dying man murmurs
from the hollow place where his echo's faint

voice is the darkness he alone travels,
as guns are primed and sweat skin becomes stone.
'Now we kill him,' and they aim their barrels.

And so I step into the line of fire,
between the dying man and the killer

whose dart gaze flickers in spits of glass flame,
a lick of heat, the hollow of dead eyes.
They are the story of what then became

those eyes, which spoke of fear, spoke of lies
turned mortal truth. They spoke the loneliness
of mothers' sons, of secrets in disguise

as myths, hush talked-of in the powerless
hungry breath of the dying man. Perhaps
the time had come. Not his, but mine, witness

turned stranger, outsider whose shadow steps
shuffle into the gaze of flame-spit eyes,
whose voice drifts into the fury that creeps

snarling through the heat. Nodding where he lies,
I hum: 'Leave him to go, before he dies.'

They fumble, brittle, like men embarrassed,
children trapped in the act of stealing treats.
The fury fades, myths fragile, words now blessed

flowing as blood along that haunted street.
'Reporter say that man should go,' one says,
calling the others, as if in defeat.

'He's going to die anyway,' I say,
stronger now, though voicing words from nowhere
I had been before that dry fragile day.

'He'll die anyway.' Seem not to care,
seem not to be all it is I might be.
Tell nothing. Pretend, just like the killer

in the guise he acts. 'You say let him free,'
one says, his searching gaze now fixed on me.

Now, there is only noise. They talk and scream.
But the man in the barrow is silent.
I catch the eye of the one who pushed him

to where we now stand, face panic, back bent
over the friend he sees he cannot save.
'Go now', I hum, the gunmen's anger spent,

as they lounge back on the deck chairs, then wave
the man away, free to push the barrow
along the street. 'Reporter. You so brave,'

one gunman smiles. 'Come back whenever
you around,' he tells me. 'I will,' I say,
and step into the sunlight, and now breathe

again, and pass the man whose life was spared.
'Thanks,' says the barrow pusher. 'Now he dead.'

Dead, in the midday sun, on the steep hill
which rises to the masonic temple
the dead man's friend is too weak and frail

to climb. 'Nowhere to go. Lost my people.
All gone now,' he says softly, to himself,
his last strength ebbing like the last ripple

on a stream bed. Dry now, ash on old breath,
silence is my footsteps pacing darkness
in stark sun. I am walking towards death.

I am walking under the sun. My legs
are running. My face is invisible.
I am running from a dead man's last words,

nowhere to go but the top of the hill.
I'm running from eyes which follow me still.

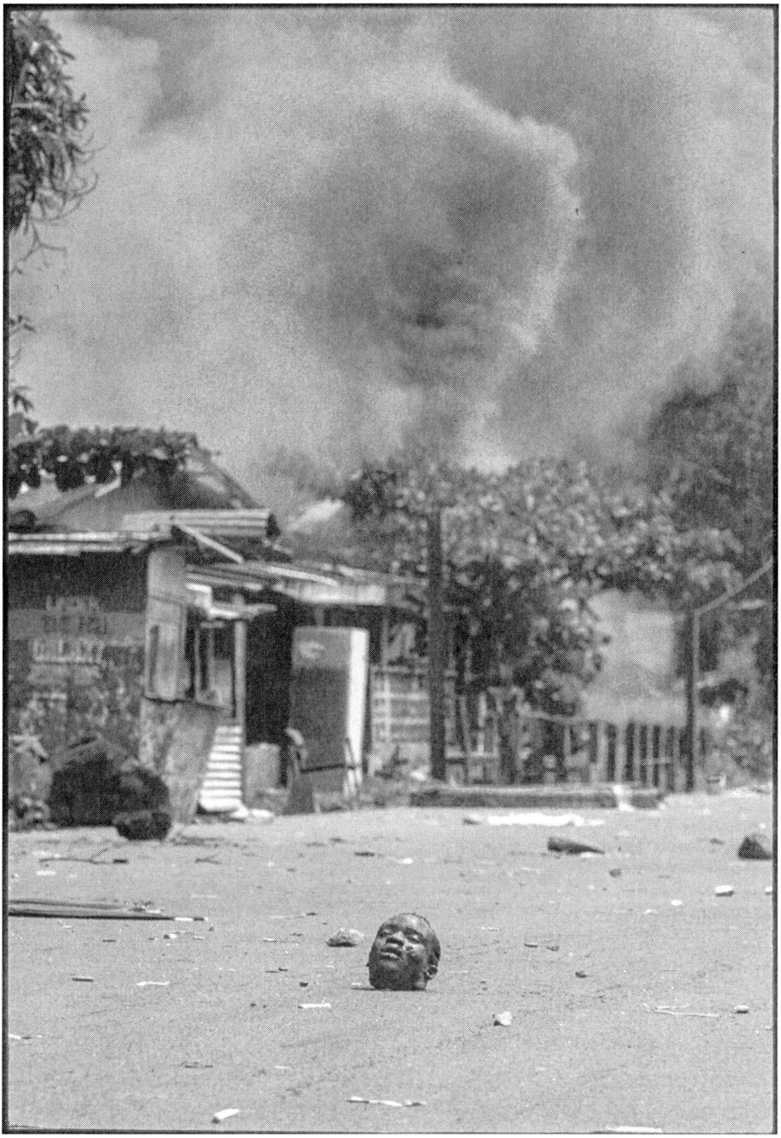

Fourth Part: The Liberator

I'm hungry on this wet August morning,
hungry as I step out onto the street
where silence voices the strangest warning

of what the night has carved beneath my feet.
I am the ghost of the one who had been
near-invisible in the morning heat,

as my steps trace the path I have seen
as a stranger whose story I'll not tell
to the one who wanders through my cold dream.

I dream of a voice that I once knew well,
but which falls silent at each word I speak,
and is gone each day when the hard rains fall

upon the story on which I now wake
alone with silence a lone bird could break.

*

In a mud slag pit beside the river
the trash of the war rusts bullets and blood,
and a dog tears parched flesh from a trouser

which binds a dead man's bones. We in silence,
we drive across the People's Bridge, the flood
beneath its span a cobbled track of backs

and heads, at peace now from the war. The dead
are watching me, eyeing from the mangrove
all who pass. Any moment I will tread

among death's strewn debris. Abdullah drives
fast, covers his mouth and nose, horrified
that those were the people whose lives once wove

the city's days and nights. 'Hard to believe',
he murmurs. 'This my home. It be my grave.'

Heavy rain drowns the island's hollow light.
This is Bushrod, where the dark emptiness
of homes and factories stares as blank as night

onto the echo as our car creeps past.
We find him, strumming a two-string guitar
on the roof of a skeleton car, dressed

in the rank of an army officer,
his guard of armed men and boys lounging slouched
on settees, cheering The Liberator

as the city's fleeing people sit crouched,
evading the blood-shot eyes and ice stare
of Prince Johnson as he sings of lives touched

by love. And the silent crowd knots its fear
as the hard rains ease and the sky scrapes clear.

Like a thief found stealing a big idea,
I follow at speed his convoy's rampage
through the ruins. Empty as a stranger,

I am an actor on a theatre stage
I am a pretender whose face is stone
and am words once read on a long-dead page.

Now I follow The Leader's procession
like a believer on a Judgement Day,
a lost child lured by a piper's tune,

onward into tomorrow. The dead lie
savaged on the copper earth we drive past,
sculpted raw and naked as the trophy

landscape shaped when a loaded die is cast
and each moment is breathed which is the last.

I follow the men who split the city,
who fought their way through the darkest forest,
a faction split from the rebel army.

In a red-brick chalet out to the west
where Stockton Creek drifts at the garden's edge,
they gabble and punch their tales as best

as they can tell, these men and boys whose pledge
to Prince their Leader is voiced by tears.
Men cry. In hope, despair. The tears they shed

are diamonds in squint eyes which betray fears
long-hiding the secrets of their hunger.
Old men cry, as boys aged beyond their years

drag the child in them beneath the thunder
and bury its bones where stray dogs wander.

'He bring us to the Promised Land, he will,'
a bone-cheeked old man rasps in words which crack
the heavy load of morning's heat. 'He will

deliver us, our Prince.' But the boys smirk,
embarrassed by the old man's devotion.
'Come, old man,' one says, as young smiles break

on children's faces, and celebration
sounds through the chalet door. 'Come, drink beer,'
a voice calls, as Prince steps into the sun.

'Bring me those looters. Bring them all here,
right now.' Three boys are forced to strip and lie.
Drunk, Prince kicks their heads as they scream in fear

and plead innocence and that truth can lie,
knowing this day they neither live nor die.

And I watch, like the people on the street,
an eye on the smile on Prince's face,
a glance at the red earth beneath my feet.

Then Prince strides back inside, and the bleeding
boys shift and crawl, their young bodies broken
but their hearts alive, their legs now limping

towards the gate which the sentries open
onto the broken city. And inside
men tap at typewriters, drafting statements

for an ultimatum, while there beside
a window at a large polished pine desk
Prince adjusts a blotter and grins with pride

swigging from a can as I think to ask:
'Can it ever end, what has come to pass?'

But his rasp voice talks only of revenge.
He stutters laughter. A coyote grin.
A wolf's snarl, as cracked fingers now arrange

miniature flags and a device that spins
across the polished desk, as his words dry
and the typists tap. A new world begins

and ends in the blink of a blood-shot eye
now staring hard at me. 'You reporters.
You write the truth now. Tell no lie,' and I

see him kicking heads, hear pleading looters
beg a day before their execution.
I see copper-red earth suck blood water

and stare at the face of liberation,
and hear the voice of desolation,

the voice of a man I might one day trace,
the one who lives as a stranger in me,
the one whose dreaming brought me to this place

which is now my home, an imaginary
place no one ever imagined for me.
There is a city beside the salt sea

where only by chance I found I could be
the stranger alone who nobody knows,
whose wandering shadow has been set free.

Who is the boy, that young stranger who goes,
showing no fear when the storm clouds burst?
But terror is eating me. No one knows

the hunger inside is parching my thirst,
here in this land, where old nightmares rehearsed.

But there's safety where the typewriters tap,
where the coyote grins and the wolf snarls
from The Liberator's face. Torn boots slap

the marble, and that lair of yellow walls
is warm with voices. There is no danger
there. It is safe where the crisp cockroach crawls

into the air-conditioning grille, safer
than the street, the Bridge, or the place I stay.
I am safe here among the killers,

until the last word's said and I'm away
from there and back under the blinding rain

never really knowing what part I should play,
promising Prince I'll come back there again,
across the Bridge to the rebel domain.

*

Then, out on the street, everything has changed.
The People's Bridge has become the front line,
the mangrove swamp where the dead are arranged

on the tides, laps and heaves, air salt with brine,
light dragging wet heat as shots spit and crack
with the snap of bone. The street's mirror sheen

captures great white clouds, which stroll the dark back
of the swirling drifting Mesurado.
We crouch trapped by the gunfire, down a track

of mud between shacks. We cannot follow
nor retrace the route which had led us there,
the battle for the Bridge howling below

where we'll wait in the rain until we dare
leave the dry shadows now hiding us there.

'Go. Go now. You can go,' a small sweat-face boy
yells, rifle gripped, hands gloved, cowrie headband
bound tight. 'Go. Bridge safe now.' And Abdullah

edges the car out from the red-earth sand
and into the glare of the battlefield
road which curves the swamp and the empty land.

To cross the Bridge to the distant far side.
There is no reason. But the engine wails
and the bullet earth grinds as the car glides

between water and sky. A small boat's sails
ride the river mouth's swell, as gunfire cracks
the heavy wet air ragged from nails

which rip our molten breath, and burn their tracks
through bodies in the grip of hunter's traps,

in a place with no beginning nor end,
on a road I cannot see, on a bridge
across a river whose name I once said.

This place which is nowhere, poised on the edge
of a space between, is water and sky
and fire and ice, now burning the cage

the world has become. My eyes do not cry,
my fear is stone, the hate of the heat
now freezes my bones. I am mystery

told on a long-dead page, words to repeat
without beginning or end. A story
might one day be read, of death where a street

crossed a bridge to a city on salt sea.
The dead then long-gone. The dead are not me.

The moments crawl, and our car grinds towards
a far distance which is both life and death.
The space between silence and final words

is a bridge carving its place on the earth,
a space torn from a low sky of grey salt,
where our crippled car now catches its breath

against the wall of Waterside Market,
its stalls crushed to rubble where dog packs scowl,
teeth bared. The dogs are dying, skin cracked,

torn from ribs like the men's bodies they maul.
I watch, as claws scratch the blood of the street,
and press myself against the wet brick wall,

smelling the fear, my shirt it smells sweet
as the carcass which lies dead at the feet

which step to carry me. I move. I drift
among tenements rotting in the rain,
leave Abdullah and his car by a path

hidden as a secret, and reach the lane
where I once saw a man torn from his home,
whose children never saw Papa again.

Ahead, a man runs fast in day's hot sun.
He sometimes brings me information,
but breathless now he gasps as if the one

last word he speaks of 'the situation'
he always called the war, will turn morning
to night. Catch breath. Speak. And where sun once shone

he tells of slaughter in a church, saying
that even President Doe strode hiding

behind a mask among the bodies there,
as his death-squad murdered through the night,
and in the morning thirsted still for more.

Saint Peter's Church was where the babies cried
in mothers' arms and soldiers rattled gates
to terrify the people crammed inside.

But when Tilly the Killer chose their fate
and the pews and alter ran thick with blood,
the ritual horror that masked men create

turned morning cold on the street where I stood
listening to my informant's nightmare tale.
That place where the screams of children still flood

the hollow night and raped women wail –
I must tell the world of its betrayal.

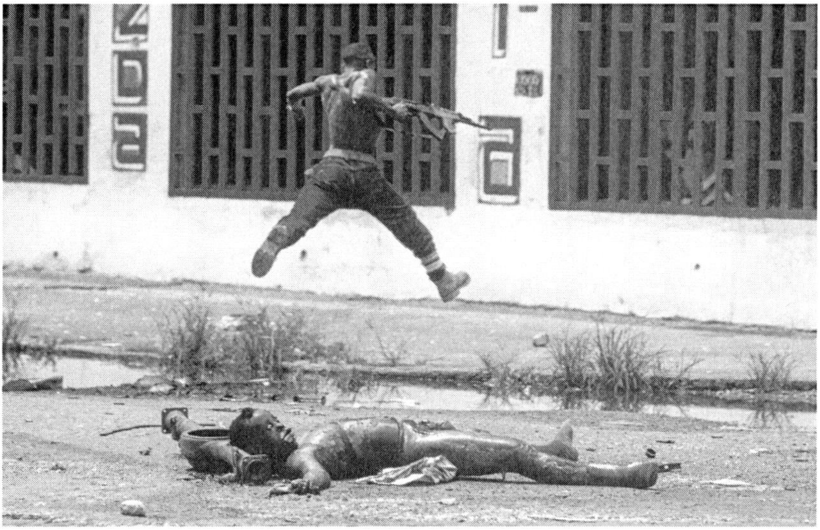

Fifth Part: A midsummer morning

The morning of August 12 is quieter
in the city. These days I barely speak
with the two old agency reporters

whose house I share. Sometimes, when tempers break,
they sneer at this outsider with no cash
to feed himself, who wanders through the streets

of war, aimless as a scrag dog on trash-
heaps smouldering by shacks. But now the ghost
of dawn spins the waves' rolling hush

beyond the palm stumps. This will be the last
of the days spent watching two armies drift
between the destined border and time past.

As now, the midnight mask they would not lift
has slipped like wrapping from a poisoned gift.

In the rising heat, Abdullah drives us
through the streets which for weeks I've walked alone.
The window damps the echoing silence

humming emptiness through where I belong,
out there beyond the cracked and smeared glass.
We drive streets where sometimes I heard a song,

The Prisoner, wailing loud. Now we pass
a place where once two men died at my feet,
where a man wheeled his dead friend up past

children tearing limes from a tree, the sweet
fruit rotten, their laughter their tragedy,
as rhyme games were played out there on the street

near where the whores on their balcony
stare as we pass without waving at me.

Abdullah will drive no further, and stops
his car where the slope of Crown Hill starts its
rise through No-Man's Land. There, the motor cuts

and silence floods the city's emptiness.
Prince Johnson's boys linger in the doorway
of a fire-scarred shop, a concrete staircase

rising to nowhere up beside the grey
blocks of a charred wall. A man, part-eaten,
is splayed on the steps, Icarus at play

after the fall, a long fall, to sweeten
the sunlight which shadows the crippled wings
of a man who fell, whose dream was beaten

by the song of the Devil as he sings
of monstrous witches and prophets and kings.

*

We step from the car and stare up the hill,
the road we must take to the other side.
We imagine, perhaps imagine still,

the outsider's hope, on feet that will glide.
There is no war for us. We are just words,
telling the tales of a world so wide

our stories of war are all that we heard.
But when we step into the silent place
between the men who live by guns and swords,

we are nowhere. A drift of smoke through space,
Prince Johnson's boys murmuring at our backs,
the brittle tarmac counting every pace.

We can't turn, nor look to retrace our tracks,
so we count our steps as if time now ticks

up the slope of the road, where the hill's brow
hides what might lie over the other side.
An unknown, a crusted shell sucked hollow

on a dead land parched by its suicide.
The empty road is bone draped with taut skin,
its gaping brow a mouth we step inside,

our footsteps the ticking moments passing.
We know we are wrong. We know we must turn.
But our rapid footsteps keep us moving

up the rising road, as the seconds burn
like nightmare's dark flooding dawn as it flows.
But dawn is darkness in the blazing sun,

where a ghost-scream cracks and an old dog scowls
among shot-riddled huts where a soldier prowls.

They crouch, a pack, in the shadows of shacks,
across wasteland at the top of Crown Hill.
Deep voices yell then the gunfire cracks

like the ripping of glass. They're with me still,
those wasteland moments and the empty road
falling behind. Run. Run back to the wall,

run, hide, and forget all I might have owed
to the story I had once come to tell.
Turn back from where the Mesurado flowed.

But I cannot turn, so stand on level
ground facing them. I cannot turn the back
they will tear if I run like a rebel,

will rip with fire on a blood-dry track
as they eye the prey they lust to attack.

Then they're upon us, sniffing around us,
shooting the sky and strutting the wasteland,
where a gouged body lies rotting in grass

and the eyes of men are red as the sand.
We are surrounded, imprisoned, now trapped.
They shove and tear and punch scabious hands,

roaring and screaming, our faces are slapped
in long dreamed-of revenge, our glasses torn,
our blurred eyes blind like the prisoner who slept

through time until execution day's dawn,
when his crippled wings snapped as his life fell
from his open palms to where mothers mourn.

We are children here, three men in a cell
where no one will hear the story we'd tell.

'Damn fuckin Americans. Damn fuckin.
Damn fuckin Americans. You. You. Damned.
You damned Americans. You. Damned fuckin.'

A fist is clenched, a fist in a gloved hand,
fingers torn through holes in a soiled rag,
fingers scored and scarred from working the land.

'Gonna take you to the swamp.' His words drag
across the wasteland of zinc-sunlight rooves,
words which hold back time as stone seconds lag

and become moments which no promise proves
no knowledge shapes, which all kind words could harm.
'Take you to the swamp.' No gesture can soothe

the rage of the hand now gripping my arm
shoving me to where the water is calm,

where mangrove rises lush from the darkness,
where the river lulls the children's Papa,
who lies long-gone in the swampland's stillness.

'Take you to the swamp,' yells the same soldier,
short, squat, both young and old, both boy and man,
obsessed, mesmerised by his own power.

'Damned fuckin spies. You damned American.'
I tell him we are all from England,
a lie. 'Damned fuckin spies,' he yells again.

A taller soldier, quiet, bearded,
is perhaps his senior. He stands, watches,
says nothing. I catch his eye, and wonder.

'Empty your pocket' – the other snatches
all I take out, pen, pocket knife, then wrenches

shirts from our backs. 'Take you to the river.'
He rams my shoulders with his rifle butt.
'Go.' But I hold the eye of the other

silent soldier. He will save us, will cut
in now to tame our executioner.
But he says nothing, as sun and sweat

sting the wasteland from where we will last stare
out across the day when the judgement comes,
the killer spewing the rage and despair

of the loneliest man's desperation.
That is the horror. This is the horror,
hungry men clawing at desolation.

All horror there, in the stench of our fear
that death will come beneath a sky so clear.

*

An engine breaks through the soldiers' voices,
breaks the hum of these ever-turning worlds.
A yellow cab halts where Crown Hill crosses

the wasteland which is the battlefield
where we now sit forced down on the kerbstone.
'Bare-foot. Bare-foot,' the same soldier bellows.

Bare-foot, bare-backed under the midday sun,
the taxi motor turning, like comfort.
And we three silent, together alone,

as strange to each other as those we fight
with words and signs and our empty steps.
'Get inside.' And we cram bare-backed bare-foot

into the dust-oil stench and stale sweat
of the taxi, which crawls the emptiness.

And after seconds or hours we stop
outside a building, where plaster lions
snarl pock-marked as they guard a grand entrance.

Once, many months before, I went in there,
to obtain a card from the Minister,
permission to be in Liberia,

making life easy for the visitor.
Soldiers run up to the taxi window.
'Damned fuckin Americans,' they splutter

and scream. Fists punch, rifles aim, moments slow
to paralysed. The engine cuts silent
and last words are of a place I might know,

where all that was said was not what was meant,
there where the lions carve out their lament.

Nothing is said nor any sound stuttered,
in this dreadful place of preparation,
where a homeland sparrow chirps then flutters

like life in a place skinned of all motion.
We are waiting. We wait. We are waiting
for a moment which may be salvation.

Let this end. I am no longer waiting.
A wide empty road unbroken by war.
There is no blood, just some men now sitting

in a hot car. What are we expecting
will scatter the hate we have created?
Can I kill to live? I saw men killing.

Will I be living when this day is dead,
when the heat is gone, and the last word said?

I imagine I am invisible,
nobody. The car now moves – across land
which has poisoned agony's crucible,

forged from a hollow by a rag-skin hand.
I imagine I am the twilight star,
glaring cold-eyed at a city which stands

where the ocean's edge sings to Africa.
I hear it now, that distant thunder
of the waves, the churning of the water

beyond the Barclay Camp cowering under
the storm-cloud sky. Now a barrier slammed
as we drive through, brings us where the murder

of men hid its face as the ocean screamed,
and haunted the living as children dreamed.

*

The salt-spray sucks at our wind-parched lips
as a shadow orders us to follow
up steps to a room where a brass tap drips

to country music on a radio.
In his office Lieutenant-Colonel Wright
murmurs, curious, saying we must go

to see the General, to hear what he might
decide to do with these reporter men.
We follow through darkness and through the light

of rooms where the names of dead men remain
etched in dust-encrusted futility,
and drift past rooms where failed plans have lain

on the moulding maps of a strategy
which the hunters drowned in a blood-red sea.

'If our men have treated you badly,
then I am sorry,' the General smiles.
'I am truly sorry, I am, truly,'

he insists, as he holds out two big hands
to shake. 'I welcome you to the barracks,'
he adds, nodding, while his deputy fans

the flies with a brown file lying stacked
on a neatly-ordered desk with the name:
'Gen. Hezekiah Bowen' carefully stamped

on black plastic. 'Is it true that you came
from rebel side?' his young deputy's head
tilts with a grin, and so our time became

a story not lived but a story read
when the sunset warns of black nights ahead.

And so we laugh at all that might have passed,
the General a little sterner when asked
to tell of what took place a few day's past

at Saint Peter's Church. Then his face is cast
in stone, his friendly eyes now glazed despair,
as he listens calmly to all we ask

about what exactly had happened there.
But he will not say, perhaps does not know.
His army was weak, we would later hear,

and the death-squad were men who did not show
their faces. 'Yes. There's been indiscipline,'
he says, standing, as if a sign to go,

a desperate man whose terrible sin
was to have seen the skull beneath the skin,

which sweats at his soft palms as we step out
of the clammy room and into salt sun,
where the shadow faces don't sneer or shout,

but stare cold, as a sentry swings his gun
and releases the twisted rusting bar
we walk beneath in silence, and then turn

towards the frontline down at the corner.
There's an old soldier there, in a manhole.
'Gonna get 'em. Damned rebels,' his murmur

an epitaph for the city's dead soul,
whose grinning mouth speaks from the grave it's dug
where cemetery bones brush the barracks wall,

and we leave him there in his hole so snug,
and claw at the silence of night's ice drug.

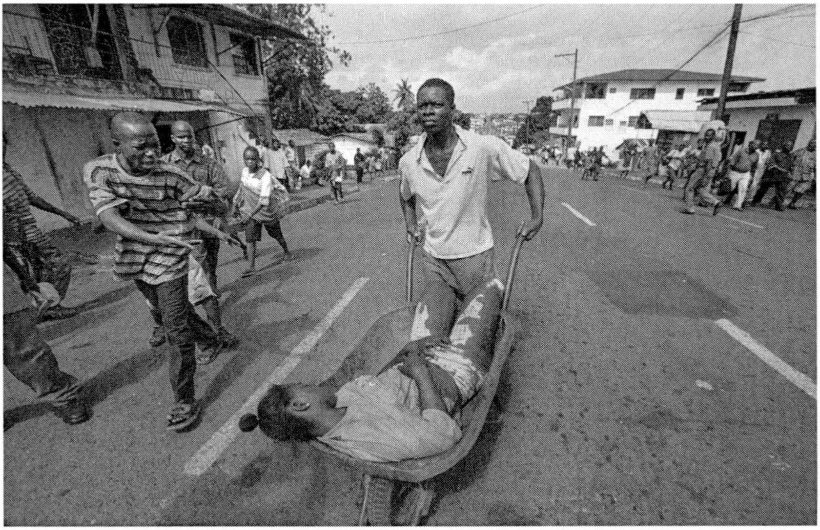

Sixth Part: The executioner

A helicopter skimmed the peeling surf.
The forest smothered the land, dense as hair.
I had run from that place, had lost my nerve,

had run far away from what I'd seen there,
run to hear voices in other places,
fled from the iron of Monrovia's stare.

But it followed me in haunted faces,
till aboard a great ship I travelled back,
surging the ocean of empty spaces

whose voices roared hollow at my raw back.
And I clung to grip in desperation,
to what might lie ahead beyond the black

night our ship sailed, beneath stars which shone
their metal course to that destination.

It is autumn now, where I used to live,
that place I once was, so far to the north.
I have nothing to live for, nor to give,

cradled by night at the end of the earth,
where through the darkness I hope not to wake,
but dream of the landscape that was my birth.

Three nights at sea, on the fourth day we make
for the coast, where the torn city's skull gapes
as we edge closer to where salt waves break

at the harbour wall and a ripped flag drapes
the port in a ghost dream of nationhood.

There, I stand between the empty landscapes,
the ocean a haven drowned in the flood,
the city a creature drained of its blood.

Just like a traveller, one passing through,
me and the war are a memory now.
It saw me arrive and watched as I grew,

then it released me, but won't let me go.
Soldiers had come from across foreign lands
to bring peace to the streets we now drive slow,

among people who shift shapeless as sands.
There is movement now, where once there'd been rain,
and the drifting of life where the Bridge stands

with its open palm soft where there'd been pain.
But there in the eyes, where daylight runs cold,
all that has passed is again what remains

of that time the story of war was told
by those who were there before they grew old.

*

Fatter now, behind his big wooden desk,
Prince Johnson welcomes me as a lost friend.
It's been a month since I was last his guest

in that villa where his office staff send
press releases on the situation
to diplomats eager to understand.

Beer in fist, there's an invitation
then issued to everyone in that hot house
to watch a movie 'for recreation'.

'D'ya wanna see my film?' Prince asks us,
with a grin which might have been a smile,
and we follow out onto the terrace

where children play before they wait a while
as chairs are scraped across the mottled tiles.

A faded image on a TV screen
flickers then rolls as a silence falls
along Stockton Creek, where the drifting stream

is all that moves where a sparrow now calls.
'D'ya wanna see my film?' the question rings
as on the screen between the moulding walls

of that office room where a man now sings,
President Doe sits on the floor, stripped
but for his underwear. A firm hand brings

the camera close to a face scarred and whipped
with glass, blood where hair is ripped from his head.
Arms bound tight he begs through his swollen lips

for the mercy a man might show instead
to the fallen chief of the living dead.

Once again there is that voice I know, the rasp
of orders issued from those grinning lips,
solemn rituals breathless men now grasp

with hands which the Country Devil now grips.
'I'm a humanitarian,' says Prince,
then: 'Cut off one ear,' and a knife slips

from a sheath and a steel blade now glints
among the arms and feet that hold Doe down.
His scream fills the world. But there are no hints

of horror on the faces there, no sound
nor shame nor sickness at the tyrant's pain,
and only silence when Doe's ear is found

and handed to Prince as the victor's gain,
and bitten on film in the ritual game.

Now the President sits up, his head bowed,
the heat in that room raging in voices
frightened excited, a hatred unbound

by victory's gift of savage choices.
Doe shakes his head, a dying man, and blows
down across his chest as rebel faces

smirk at the spell he casts from mouth and nose.
'He blow to make himself disappear,'
a voice behind me says, as murmurs rose

among the audience there. Then the fear
wracks Doe's bloodied face, a man now naked
on the lawn by this terrace, and we hear

the Creek slipping by in words left unsaid,
as nightmares are forged and hunger is fed.

Prince's film flickered to a silent end
and I stood, numb as a child still-born,
stone as a lie which no face could pretend

to the bodies now moving to the room
where these people knew a thing once happened,
where the killer's craft honoured that oath sworn

in the darkness where the forest trees stand,
there where the loyal boy became a man,
where rotting life poisoned that dying land.

And I drift like dawn on a sea of sand,
no words to speak nor offering to make
to Prince and his boys as I shake that hand,

which grips mine so hard as if made to break
the bones which will hold the pen I'll take.

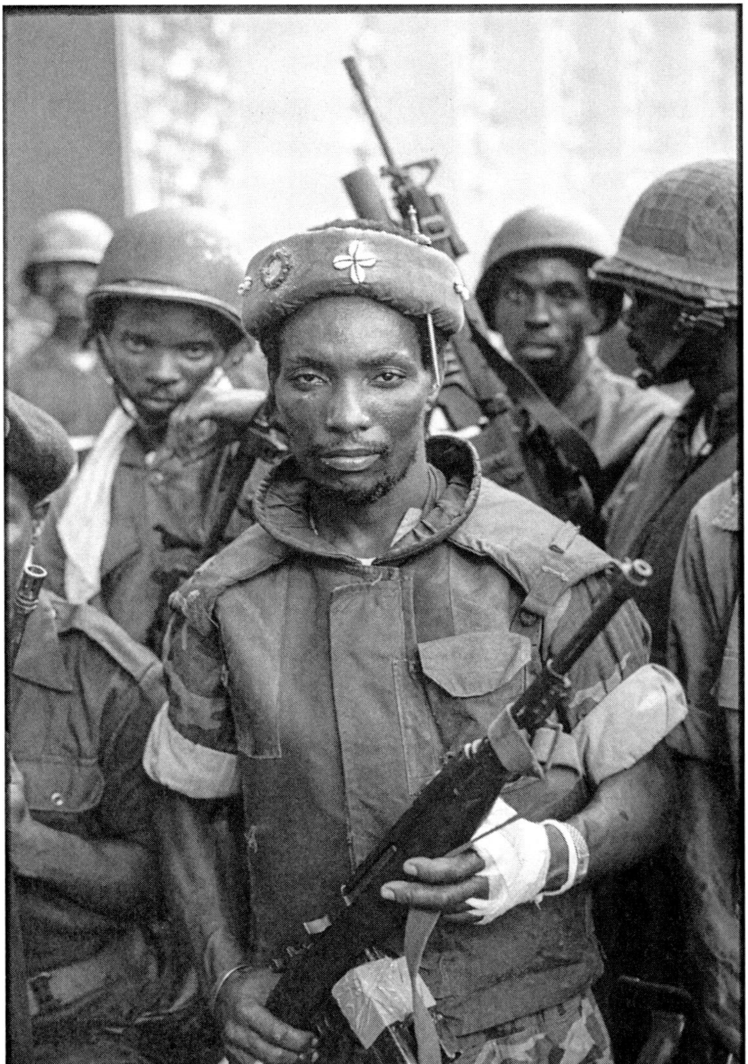

Epilogue

I left my home with no tale to tell
of the places my lonely dream-time drifts,
as one whose story casts the strangest spell

turning brutal truths to fragile myths.
I never imagined Monrovia –
a place on a map where the mangrove shifts –

till it lost its secrets and its saviour,
and I stumbled to where our two paths crossed
in a storm in a land like no other,

where true myths became what the killers' cost.
Now the poisoned streets writhe as our truck drives
among shadow times of memory's ghost,

rising Crown Hill and past where three men's lives
became the words of the one who survives.

We pass along streets where the death-squads prowled
until the slaughter was too much to bear,
so troops marched in where militiamen scowled

at the foreigners who now speed through there.
In the city a truce let me across
the frontline where the two lions still stare,

scarred and cracked and guarding all that is lost
when a nation tears the heart from its breast.
As if nowhere in the city we've crossed,

where once were borders can only be guessed,
as a steeple rises beside the street,
and golden sun falls somewhere to the west,

and we stop where a path and wet road meet,
where the soft sound is the running of feet.

Nobody dares to look at Saint Peter's Church,
the place we tried to reach that August day.
There's a killer on the loose who will come in search

of curious kin who might pass that way.
I push open the gate the killers chained,
and step up the path where the grass stems sway,

then pass through the door where the step is stained
a red-brown sheen in the gold of the sun.
But there inside, sun's light has been drained.

Bodies drape the pews, their sinews skin spun
parched tight where mothers still clutch suckling lips
poised to drink from the barrel of a gun.

The floor ripples as a maggot sea sips
at death's ripe feast, then outside gunfire rips

the afternoon sky which had been so still,
and voices yell as if the war had come.
Beyond the gate they are ready to kill

all who might steal the prize they had won,
the rotting trophy lying at my feet
a secret truth they'd share with no-one

but the potent chief no man can defeat.
And he stood there now, Tilly the Killer,
the death-squad leader whose name none repeat,

there he watched and stared, the famed young hunter
whose crimes tore to pieces the country's soul.
'You, actors. Actors,' he snarled, a winter

freeze in dead eyes which crawled as dark as coal
into the folklore which dare not be told.

In another life, Tilly might have been
some other young man of no consequence.
But there in the rain, beside that crime scene,

he was animal life living by chance.
I had seen all that I should not have seen,
had trespassed in the citadel to glance

for a moment where I should not have been,
and now acted my innocent pretence.
But he knew, when he asked: 'What ha' you seen?'

and I stared back hard and kept my silence
as his gang murmured awkward then just glared
as we drove away into a distance

which became days and months of nightmares snared
by moments on those same streets I once shared

with killers whose dreams some would later tell
were the faces of all those they had killed.
One told me then he is visited still,

by the masked dead where in a room he willed
in a dream they would all come back to life.
Just a boy of 12 in his own dark hell,

haunted by wounds that he cut with his knife.

LIVE CANON